I0488691

# LEARN HOW TO MANAGE AND MARKET YOUR BUSINESS ONLINE REPUTATION

By
Randy Walden

# Table of Contents

# Why is Your Online Reputation Important?

*"A good reputation is more valuable than money."*
*Publilius Syrus*

In a survey posted by BrightLocal.com in August of 2015 the reported these important findings:

- 92% of consumers now read online reviews (vs. 88% in 2014)
- 40% of consumers form an opinion by reading just 1-3 reviews (vs. 29% in 2014)
- Star rating is #1 factor used by consumers to judge a business
- Star rating is #1 factor used by consumers to judge a business
- 68% say positive reviews make them trust a local business more (vs. 72% in 2014)

As a business owner it is important for you to pay attention to your business's online reputation. What exactly is your online reputation? Basically, it is the impression your company gives and what people think of you when they're surfing the Web. But your online reputation is much more than just that. Just like your reputation offline, your online rep is something that you can easily control.

Do you really know what your online reputation is? Do you know what customers are saying about you and your product or your service? Do you know how to fix it if there is bad publicity out there about your company? Most importantly, do you know how to protect your online reputation from being tarnished?

There are now thousands, even millions of ways for complete strangers to communicate and talk to each other online. Without your knowledge, these people could be posting negative comments about your company, writing negative reviews about your product or service, talking up your competition, or possibly even creating a hate site regarding you and your company. How does this affect you?

The first and most obvious way is that other customers could see this and be turned away from your product or company based on just one thing they see online. But there's even more to worry about than the possibility of losing a single customer. What if a business partner saw a review posted on your alleged bad business practices? You could lose investors and maybe even future income should that partner be so put off by what they saw that they pull out of your company. What if prospective employees researched your company and decided not to apply because they read a negative blog post posted by a former, angry employee? You could lose a great asset for your company simply due to a disgruntled employee.

Yes, your company's online reputation affects it and everything it does. Once you really stop and think about it managing, protecting, and building your business' online reputation can be a pretty messy matter. But it doesn't have to be. There are plenty of resources out there that are available to help you and your company and this report is one of them. Taken step by step, your business's online reputation *can* be managed, protected and built into what you need it to be.

# Assessing your Online Reputation

*"One can survive everything nowadays, except death, and live down anything, except a good reputation."*
*Oscar Wilde*

Before you can start doing anything with your online reputation – fixing it, building it, doing anything to it – you first need to know what your online reputation is. But how do you find that out? The only way is to assess your reputation, but how exactly are you supposed to do that?

## How to Assess Your Online Reputation

It's easy, really. Just search for your company online and see what you find. Make sure to check the results of different search engines. The different engines have different requirements for keywords and different ways to search for information. Because of that, you need to make sure that you're searching not only general search engines such as Google, Yahoo, TripAdvisor, and MSN; but also the metasearch engines such as Info.com, Dogpile, and WebCrawler.

So what should you be searching for? Your name is an obvious one, especially if you're the CEO or the President of a company; and you've probably already guessed that you should search for your company name as well. It is a good idea to also search for your brand, your product, your employees (especially those that deal with the public a lot,) and any usernames that you may use in association with your business.

Also remember while you're searching for information on your company that search engines are commonly personalized right now, meaning that the results you see will probably be based on your location, as well as customized results should you or your company be signed into that particular search engine. For example, if you're signed into Google and search for your own company name while you're signed in, you may only get to see results of material you've written, or material that you already know is out there. What you want to find is the material you *don't* already know about and that could be negatively affecting your business.

Also be sure to search social networks, such as Facebook and Twitter. While Facebook might be a bit trickier to find (especially once you've wandered off your own profile or business page), Twitter will be very easy. Simply type in your keywords into Twitter's search box and it will provide you with a listing of the most recent tweets made about you, your company, and your product or services.

Once you've done some searching and found some results, what are you supposed to do with them? You need to track them! Create a spreadsheet that you can reference at any time and put the following information on it, in this order: position in the search engines (was it the first, second, fourth, etc. result); the URL that has the publicity; the type of publicity (whether it's good, bad, indifferent, or not about you); and the general sentiment behind the posting. Perform a search on each keyword (your name, your company's name, etc.). As you search, record the first 30 results that you found on your spreadsheet, regardless of the sentiment behind them.

## The Three Biggest Online Reputation Problems

Once you've done this you've assessed your online reputation! Now all you have to do is look over your results and determine the overall outlook of that reputation. What you'll be looking for during your research are these three problems:

- Results that are shown but are not about you or your company.

- Results that are shown that *are* regarding your company, but are indifferent.

- Results for your company that show negative comments and remarks.

While this latter problem is an obvious one, why does it matter if there are indifferent results about your company or if the results are not about you?

If you search through the first 30 results and none of them are about you (or not the majority of them,) it means you don't really have much of an online reputation. Why is this a problem? Well for starters, it means that people don't think anything about you, good or bad. They may not even know that your company exists! And that's a problem. The bigger problem with not having an online reputation is that when other people want to post something negative about your company, they can, and they might even quickly climb to the top of the page rankings in the search engines with that bad review or comment. This means that when anyone searches your company, the first thing they'll see is that negative comment. In short, if you don't build your own online reputation yourself, someone will do it for you.

Although less common, sometimes people can't find you through a search because you share the same name with a company, a celebrity, or someone else that's very high-profile. In this instance, when people search for your company they might find a long list of results that have that name, but those results still won't be specific to your company. In this case, you need to also include other keywords that could narrow the search down more – adding your location, your product, or your industry could help with this and could refine the search for both you and your customers. This is still something you need to take very seriously because when people aren't finding you online, you can still consider yourself as having an indifferent online reputation. People don't search farther than the first page or two in the search engines. And if you're way back at the 30th page, they're never going to find you.

Along with negative comments being found, or people not finding you at all, another big problem that you might run into with your online reputation is that while there are lots of results, they might be indifferent. So, how does a result that's neither good nor bad negatively affect you? It's because people who are searching for your company need to know more than just "it's not bad," – they need to know it's *good!* A simple directory listing or a map to your place of business isn't telling the customer enough. It's not telling them why they should shop with you, what you have to offer, or how your product or service will help them. Without any real concrete reason to even click on your name, the chances are that they'll move on to your competition that has glowing testimonials, reviews, and comments in most of the results generated.

Of course, there is one more problem besides having indifferent results or results that aren't about your company. That problem is the biggest one you'll have with your online reputation – when results *are* about you, and they're bad. In that case, you're going to need to do some serious damage control in order to get your online reputation to where it needs to be. How to do that will be covered later on in this report but first, it's important you understand what *all* the possible online reputation management problems are, in addition to these biggest three.

## The Most Common Online Reputation Problems

Truthfully, there can be quite a few things online that are harming and damaging your company's online reputation. But you're likely to come across some very common ones; here are the top 10 most common problems:

- **The industry's perception of your company:** If trusted professionals in your industry don't respect you, they may be likely to say so and give negative publicity to your company. And if that's the case, customers may come across that when searching for you and they might believe what they read.

- **Scandals or salacious stories involving your company:** If your company has been involved in a scandal (tax fraud, customer disputes, etc.) even if it happened years ago and when the company was under different ownership, it could still be lurking out in cyberspace, and it could be potentially damaging for your company. Remember that what's online never *really* goes away.

- **Personal scandals:** If you or any employee in your company has been involved in any public scandal, it could also still be lurking around cyberspace; again, even if it happened years ago and the employee involved is no longer working for your company.

- **Third-party hate sites:** If you have ever had a disgruntled employee leave your company, or you've ever had a run-in with a particularly unhappy customer, it takes nothing for them to create a website and start posting all kinds of negative reviews about your company. Hate sites can be extremely detrimental to your company's reputation, so it's important that you do what you can to get them taken down as soon as you can.

- **Attacks from competitors:** If your competition doesn't believe in fair business practice and doesn't hesitate to play dirty, they may openly attack you on their own website in order to lure customers away from you and towards their business. This is something that should *never* be done and if someone is using these tactics against your company there may be legal action that you can take. The important thing is that you find these online attacks and take care of them as soon as you can.

- **Complaint sites:** Complaint sites are different from hate sites in the way that they don't have to be created by a specific individual or group that is unsatisfied with your company. Instead, they may be sites such as the Better Business Bureau or TripAdvisor, where consumers are encouraged to leave third-party reviews and testimonials of certain products and services.

When you're searching for negative reviews and comments about your company it is recommended that you also look to any organization that works with public consumers.

- **Bad press, literally:** If something hits the news the chances are good that it's going to be everywhere and that negative news story could follow your company and your online brand wherever it goes. This means that if someone is shopping for your product they could stumble upon a negative story about you or your company at the same time. Bad press is one of the most common problems businesses run into when managing their online reputation.

- **False information:** Word of mouth can be a company's best friend, but it can also sometimes be like playing the telephone game. Someone says something slightly negative about your company (or is simply misunderstood when speaking about your business) and that information gets passed from person to person. As it does, it gets changed a little each time, and that can end up with a lot of misconceptions and false information being published about your company. On the other hand, you could just have someone with a grudge against the company that publishes blatant lies. Whatever the reason for the false information, it's a big problem and it needs to be fixed immediately.

- **Squatted usernames/domain sites**: What is a squatted username or domain site? Also known as "Doppelgangers," this is a person that pretends to be you and either sets up a website or blog under your company's name, or uses your company's username on forums, in social networks, or in different chat situations. This can be a big problem for two reasons. The first, and least severe, is that you might not be able to set up a website or blog in the name you want because that name is already taken. In the worst case, the Doppelganger could, while pretending to be you, say things that are completely misrepresentative of the beliefs of you and your company.

12

While many people have not even heard of it, it is one of the most common things to negatively affect a company's online reputation. And because so few have heard about it, even more people will likely truly believe it is you posting, and not a Doppelganger.

- **Trademark infringement:** Much like Doppelgangers, people infringing on your trademark, whether they're pretending to be you or just using it without your permission, misrepresents you and can have potential customers thinking negatively about you and your brand. If your trademark is out there, and you didn't put it out there, that's negatively affecting your online reputation, and you need to fix it quickly.

Once you know what the biggest and most common online reputation management problems are, *and* you've identified where these problems lie online for your company, how do you go about fixing them? The first step is to hire a good marketing consultant who knows the ins and outs of online reputation management. And before you do that, you need to know how to go about hiring one.

# How to Hire an Internet Marketing Consultant

*"A man can get a reputation from very small things."*
*Sophocles*

Managing your online reputation, let alone all the many other things that go along with your company's online marketing strategies, can take much more time than you, as a business owner, might have. While worrying about how to turn a profit, how to reach more customers, *and* how to continually improve on your product or service, Googling your company's name and location might not be at the top of your priority list. But it doesn't have to be. Hire the right professional and you can let someone else do it all for you. All you have to do is know how to hire the right Internet marketing consultant, and to make sure that they know how to manage your online reputation.

Along with that, here are a few other things to look for:

## Hire someone that is digital savvy

This doesn't just mean hiring someone who knows how to write a blog post and publish it. The world of Internet marketing and, more specifically, managing your online reputation, requires an in-depth knowledge of things like SEO, page rankings, review sites, where comments are lurking, and where hate sites might be. You need to hire someone who not only has this knowledge, but also has a passion for this knowledge. Just as good cooks are always trying to find new recipes and new ways to improve on the old, so should an Internet marketing consultant continually be trying to learn more about the technological and online world. A professional Internet marketing consultant will always be educating themselves and keeping up with the latest in online marketing, and that includes online reputation management.

# Hire someone that is analytical

It used to be that Internet marketing consultants had to use trial-and-error methods online marketing strategies. In short, they were really just guessing at what was best for the client. If one tactic didn't work, they'd move onto another until they found one that did. When it came to managing your online reputation, they had to kind of float around in cyberspace, guessing at which sites might have information about your company, and where there might be comments and reviews about your product. Today however, you can track just about anything! How many people are visiting your site; how many people are leaving comments on your site and third-party sites; where the reviews are; the response those reviews are getting – just about anything can be tracked. Make sure you hire someone who knows how to use these kinds of tracking programs and devices – *and* who has them at their fingertips!

# Hire someone that has a great Web presence

There is no testimonial on Earth that is as good as going to an Internet marketing consultant's own website and seeing just how professional it is. This will give you a good indication as to how tech-savvy they are because you know that they've put their very best efforts into promoting themselves and that's the level you can expect from them when it comes to promoting your company. Also make sure you do a general search for the consultant in a major search engine. What results come up? Are they positive or negative? Do you find indifferent information about them, or do you have a hard time finding them? In short, try to find out what *their* online reputation is. If it's bad, that not only tells you that past clients may have been disappointed, but also that the consultant may not know how to manage their own online reputation – and that likely means that they won't know how to manage yours either.

## Employ someone that can write

Your Internet marketing consultant won't need to be able to just find reviews and fix them, they'll also need to be able to write reviews about your company and product, and they'll need to be able to write and publish blog posts and website content.

Content *is* King these days on the Internet and if your content, or content about your company or product isn't interesting, informative, and helpful, people aren't going to read it. There's simply too much out there for them to waste time reading content that won't help them. Make sure you hire someone highly experienced in online content writing, so you can be sure that any future campaigns or content written will make your customers and clients want to stick around to hear what you have to say.

# Questions to ask an Internet Marketing Consultant

*"It takes many good deeds to build a good reputation, and only one bad one to lose it."*
*Benjamin Franklin*

There will be many questions that you're going to want to ask your Internet marketing consultant. But for the purpose of this report, we'll stick to the questions you should ask your consultant, *before you hire them.* These questions will be about your online reputation and how they intend to manage it. Again, you probably have many of your own questions that you want to ask regarding your online reputation, but here are a few to get you brainstorming.

### What are the main things you will do to assess and build my online reputation?

Here you should be looking for things like searching for your company online, tracking the results they find and employing strategies to fix them. Those strategies will depend on the type of negative or indifferent results that are found and what your company needs. Many of them will be discussed in the next section – How to Build Your Online Reputation.

### What social networking sites do you use and will you use to help build my online reputation?

Things like Twitter and Facebook are a business's best friend these days. Not only can you post your own profile and even create a page for your business, but you can also track what people are saying about you. With Facebook you can do it by finding comments and replying to them. Every time someone responds, you'll be notified and you'll know how much talk your company is generating, and what that talk is. On Twitter you can utilize hashtags and set up lists to track your company and what people are tweeting about it. These are just two of the biggest social networking sites that go hand-in-hand with managing your online reputation, and your consultant needs to use these and more.

### What sites would you be using to post reviews and articles about my company and product?

Ezine, Suite 101, and Wise Geek are just a few of the sites that allow you to publish informative articles regarding your product and your company, and many will even allow a link to your website to be included in the article. The various requirements for these sites will differ, so you'll need to make sure that your consultant is familiar with them and knows which sites will get you the most results and the most positive online reputation.

### Will you write my content for me?

Having your consultant explain all those different requirements to you so that you can write your own content can cause things to once again become lost in translation. Not to mention that you probably don't have a lot of time to be sitting around writing general information articles, anyway. Make sure your consultant can do this, and that they can provide samples to prove that they have a knack for doing so.

### How will you track my online reputation?

Just like comments left on Facebook and Twitter, when you comment on a blog you can set it up so notifications are sent to you whenever someone else comments. Your consultant needs to know not only how to do this, but also how to track those results so that you can easily see and understand them. In addition to that, there are also other ways, such as Google Analytics and other tracking programs that can be employed so that you know exactly when someone is saying something about you, and what they're saying.

### If the strategies don't work, will there be any compensation?

Although there are all kinds of tracking devices and programs available to help track your online reputation, there's still no guarantee that they will work – or that the consultant employing them is knowledgeable enough to make them work. If the consultant uses all their strategies and your online reputation is still suffering (and you've likely already paid out the contract) you need to know that you will be compensated, and how. Online reputations are a difficult thing to put a warranty on, so you need to know what the consultant's policies are on failed campaigns *before* you choose to hire them.

### What digital news do you subscribe to?

Again, you need to make sure that you're hiring someone who *loves* being online and thinks there's nothing more exciting than advancements in the online and technological field. Ask them what they do to keep abreast of the current news and see how many different sources they're able to cite. That will give you an idea of just how interested they are in their field, even when they're not on the clock.

### What fees do you charge and what do those include? Will it include my online reputation management and how much priority will you give that area in online marketing?

This is a wide area and yes, just asking a marketing consultant about their fees opens the door to numerous other questions. You'll need to understand just how much time will be spent by the consultant managing your online reputation, and how much you'll be charged for that. You want a consultant that will make your online reputation a top priority, because it's really your first impression and the one chance you have to win over customers. If you find a consultant that you like but their fees are a little too high, you may want to break up certain areas of managing your online reputation and take on some of the tasks yourself. What those tasks are and what you might be able to take on yourself will be covered in the next section.

### Do you have references?

No matter how much of your online marketing the consultant is going to take over and no matter how much experience they have or how good a website, you need to make sure that they can provide you with references. Also, you need to make sure that you contact the references to find out how happy they were the consultant's services.

# How to Build Your Online Reputation

*"You can't build a reputation on what you're going to do."*
*Henry Ford*

If, after doing some searching, you find that you don't really have too much in the way of an online reputation, or even worse, that your online reputation is bad, don't panic. There are ways that you can build it and fix it. While it does take a little legwork, in the end you'll have a target audience that thinks you're *it* when it comes to your product or service. You will also find only glowing reviews and comments about you and your website when searching the Web, and that is all your customers are going to find about you too. How much of this you do yourself and how much you leave to a marketing consultant is up to you.

These are the critical steps that you must take in order to build your online reputation:

## Monitoring search engine results

We've already talked about searching for your company's name in all of the search engines, but here are some more tips to use when doing so:

- Try searching with quotes around your name and then without quotes

- Turn your location on and off.

When you are doing this you really are just assessing your reputation rather than actually building it, but it's everyone's starting point and it's imperative that you do so. You will have to continually monitor search engine results during the entire process so that you'll be able to see how your management strategies are working and if they're having any effect.

## Own your results

Ideally, you want to own every search result there is out there. If any search result comes up after someone looks up your name, you want to be in control of that site and have it say whatever you want it to. Realistically you can't own every single website that might mention your name and what may come up in the search results – but you can have some control over how many you own.

One way to do that is to build profiles – and lots of them! Whether it's a social networking site, a sharing site, your own website, or your own blog, you want to own as many of those addresses and ultimately, those search results that you can. And it's easy, you don't even need to spend a ton of money *buying* many of those addresses, you just need to create profiles. They'll be one of the first things that come up in the search results.

Here are just a few of the places where you can create a profile and one more search result in your favor:

- **LinkedIn:** Make sure you include a personal profile for yourself, as well as one for your business.

- **LinkedIn Company Page:** A relatively new feature on the professional social networking site, but one that gives you instant access to a bunch of people!

- **Google Profile:** Again, make sure that you create a personal profile for yourself, as well as one for your business.

- **Google Places account:** This is particularly important if your business has an actual physical location.

- **SlideShare:** This site allows you to give lots of visual images associated with your company and is a great way to get out photos of custom homes, designs, company logos, etc.

- **YouTube:** Again, just creating a profile on this site will put you in the top search results. Plus, you can also use this social networking site to post ads about your company, or videos and slideshows featuring your best-selling products.

- **Facebook:** this is one of the top social networking sites, to be topped only by Twitter. Most importantly, be sure you set up a fan page on Facebook for your company, or a group page for people to Like. Then create your own personal profile.

- **Flickr:** A website that's used primarily for uploading and sharing photos, this can be a great way to get the word out about corporate events, show ads for your company, or just have a "Meet the Staff" area that will let your customers know that they're dealing with friendly faces!

- **Twitter:** The #1 social networking site, you can't have an online presence and not be on Twitter. Create a profile page for your company and yourself (but most importantly your company) and then create lists so that you can answer questions, get news first and interact with people more often. Also be sure to use hash tags in Twitter so that people can easily follow you and follow as many people as you can. The more people you follow, the more your name will be out there and the more followers you'll get in return.

Creating these profiles is a huge step in building your online reputation because you're getting your name out there and you're controlling what's being said about it. Remember to always include a link back to your website or blog, so that you can increase traffic and promote yourself even further, and make sure that your profiles are being updated all the time. Information changes quickly and having a profile with the wrong information is worse than not having one at all. Also make sure that your profiles are always friendly, informative, and engaging. Again, there is a lot of competition out there and they're doing the exact same thing you are in order to attract those exact same customers. Make your page friendly and people will stick around on it a little longer.

## Track, track, and then track some more

Tracking is absolutely essential when you're trying to build your online reputation because you need to know what's being said, when it's being said, who's saying it, and where people are finding it. There are dozens of ways to track what's being said about you, here are some that you will want to employ.

- **Feed Reader:** With Feed Reader you can set up your keyword phrases and get custom feeds delivered right to you. So if you're in the refrigeration business you can set up feeds for certain refrigeration industry websites and follow them. View them regularly and see if your name comes up and if it does, what's being said about you.

- **Google Alerts:** When you find something relative to your online reputation, such as a comment or video that you find or that you uploaded yourself, you can set up a Google Alert for it. Any time there's activity on that particular piece, you'll know about it immediately.

- **Yahoo Alerts:** Similar to Google Alerts, you want to utilize Yahoo Alerts as well to keep all your search engines covered.

- **Twitter Search:** Using Twitter Search in conjunction with Twitter can help simplify your searches. With Twitter you can even perform an advanced search that will let you search for very specific things, including positive and negative information.

- **Technorati:** Technorati can be one of your biggest helpers when building your online reputation. With this tool you can set specific keywords, or your website or blog address and be notified whenever someone mentions it online.

- **BackType:** BackType will also send you notifications after you subscribe to certain keywords or your company name. BackType however, is unique in that it only searches comments so you know that an entire area of online reputation building is being done for you.

- **Social Mention:** Another tool that has a specific use is Social Mention. Social Mention, not surprisingly, is specific to social networking sites and will search conversations on those sites based on the keywords you supply. Again, you can subscribe to the feed and get alerts whenever someone brings you into the conversation.

- **BoardReader:** So you've got your social network sites down and your comments too. You still have to make sure that you're regularly checking forums and BoardReader will do that for you. This is another feed that will keep track of what's being said on forums and message boards. You can get results based on a certain date, from a certain forum, or based on relevance.

- **Yahoo Answers:** This is an interesting feed. Yahoo Answers will scour the Internet and find any questions that are being asked about you and your company. When it finds them, you can answer them and keep control of your online reputation, as well as give customers the information they need!

## Set expectations for staff and for customers

When building your online reputation, you need to know what your expectations are and what customers can expect from you. Are you going to respond to every comment? It's a good idea because it will help build your reputation, as well as help you hang onto customers. You need to let your staff know that every comment gets a response and you need to let your customers know that they'll get a response if they leave a question or a comment – you won't believe how shocked they are when they receive a response!

In addition to setting expectations for your customers, you also need to set expectations and develop guidelines and policies for your staff if they'll be involved in managing your online reputation. Will they be publishing content? Responding to comments? If so, they need to know what's considered acceptable content and what's not.

## Have more than one website

This one's really simple: the more domain addresses you own, the more you control. Buy 10 domain names with similar names and promote all of those websites and you've just taken the top 10 spots in Google. The chances that people are going to look further than that are slim and even if they do, they've already seen so much good information about your company, they'll be wary of anything negative they come across.

## Evaluate your website

So it's your website, right? You know everything that's up there and what could you possibly learn from spending a few hours looking over every link, every category, comments, and such? If you're looking carefully, you'll probably learn a lot! Are there link opportunities that are being missed? Could you be sending pingbacks and trackbacks to other sites to get your name out there once again? Are there still ex-staff members listed that should be removed? Or has the technology and information in your field changed but your website content doesn't reflect that?

Also take notice of the general look and feel of your website. Is it open and friendly to customers? Is it easy to move around between pages?

Does the site project a caring, humane presence? Is the content informative and helpful? Most of all, is it interesting?

The most important thing about your website is that it reflects who you are and has that personal touch customers are now looking for online. Tell them the story of how your company came to be, add links to the personal LinkedIn profiles of your staff members and include testimonials from past customers talking about how much your business helped them. All of this goes towards building your online reputation and one is just as important as the next.

## Find negative comments and have them removed

This one again is very simple. After hunting around and writing down the negative press that's out there about you, go back to those websites and track down the webmaster or the owner of the site. Ask them why they have the negative information up, if there's anything you can do to fix the situation, and if they'll remove the negative comments, reviews, or videos. Most of the time, those owners will be happy to do this, especially if you take the time to tell your side of the story and try to make it right. Those website owners don't want bad press or a bad online reputation, either; so they'll most likely be happy to work with you.

## Start a blog

You may have a website- you may even have 10 by now. But if you don't have a blog, you're missing out on a huge audience and a huge opportunity. Blogs differ from websites in the way that they're much more interactive with the people reading them. Your website might be full of information about your company and product, but it's just shouting that information to the customer line by line, page by page. Your blog on the other hand, is a much more casual environment in which you can regularly deliver information to your customers and provide a forum for them to discuss it, ask questions, and interact with you, as well as with other readers. Another benefit to a blog versus a website is that you can update it daily, or even more. Blogs are meant to be used as a way to bring daily updates and news to customers, whereas your website will work as a general information landing page (or pages) to tell customers about you and your product, and perhaps even give them a chance to purchase it right online.

## Issue a press release

That's right, start the presses – literally! A press release is a great opportunity to get the word out to a huge portion of the public and get them talking about your company and your product. This not only gives you a chance to tell people how great you are, but also gets people to your blog, your website, on forums, and on message boards – talking about you and your product. And the more people that know about you the more your online reputation is being built!

As you wade through these different steps (or your marketing consultant wades through them for you) you'll most likely come up with at least a few other steps you can take yourself to build, manage, and improve your online reputation. Once you've built it up to the point where you want it to be, you might think you're done. Unfortunately, that's not the case. You don't want to do all that hard work for nothing. Now you need to protect your online reputation!

# How to Protect Your Online Reputation

*"A reputation once broken may possibly be repaired, but the world will always keep their eyes on the spot where the crack was."*
*Joseph Hall*

Protecting your online reputation is important not just because of all the hard work you've done to build it up, but more importantly because you don't want anyone damaging it.

Here are some steps you can take to make sure that once you've built an online reputation for yourself, no one takes it away from you.

## Use your privacy settings

Facebook and Twitter are great things, but they can also share much more information than you ever intended. Of course, you'll only be putting up information that you want the public and customers to see, but you never know what's lurking out there and what people can see. There also might be information that you want only certain people to see, such as you're your friends or people who follow your business page. Twitter is less advanced when it comes to the privacy settings, but there may also be less information you're sharing due to character restrictions and such. LinkedIn has one of the most advanced privacy settings, giving you control over what types of information is shown to the general public, which fields show up in the search engines, or whether your profile shows up at all.

## Identify and prevent problems before they occur

As you build your online reputation you will have to keep track of more sites, profiles and domain names. The more you're out there, the better; and resources such as Google and Yahoo Alerts will be a huge help. But always, always make sure that you're scouring the Web, doing the same searches you did when analyzing your online reputation, and using different social media management systems (outlined next) to make sure that if there's a problem, you know about it. That's the only way that you can fix it – immediately.

## Social media management

Managing all of your different Twitter accounts, Facebook accounts and LinkedIn profiles can be quite a job. Luckily, there are many tools at your fingertips that can help. HootSuite and EasyTweets are two tools that you can use to manage all of your different Twitter accounts while Ping.fm will take all of your tweets and publish them to all your different social networking profiles. Disqus will keep track of all of your comment threads for you; and Atom Keep will update all of your different social networking profiles at the same time. SocialStream on the other hand, is a kind of Super Power when it comes to social media management, consolidating all of your social networking profiles into one.

## Create your own negatives

Managing your online reputation means not having one single bad word out there about you and your company, right? Well, not necessarily. You can actually buy a domain name such as "yourcompanysucks.com" and use it to your advantage. The first advantage of this tactic is that you're not leaving that domain name out there for some disgruntled employee or unsatisfied customer to create.

Second, it's an invitation for your customers to tell you exactly what they think sucks about you – and yes, that's a good thing. It gives you one last chance to appeal to that customer, show them that you care, and that you want to fix the problem. Make a cute landing page like,

"Hi! Tell us why we suck!" Then leave an open forum for people to leave complaints or ideas on how you could improve your product or service.

Beware- with this comes a word of warning. Yes, you want to make your customers feel as though they're welcome to offer constructive criticism, but you should never allow swearing, threatening, rude behavior, or anything else offensive on your site. It needs to be general public-friendly and make people feel as though it's a place to speak and be heard, not speak and be tormented. And you shouldn't have to put up with any torment, either. After all, it's your site. You control the content. And allowing horrible comments to be left up is not going to improve your online reputation.

## Listen to constructive criticism

Remember that if you set up a site for your customers to complain and voice concern, you need to listen to them when they do just that. Getting defensive and angry isn't going to help you. Listen to what customers have to say and try to think of a way that you can help them. Respond to them kindly and humanely and try to offer them something in return. The chances are that if you can remain cool-headed you'll win the angry customer over and they'll end up liking you because you've gone so far out of your way to correct a bad situation for them.

## Build credibility

Building credibility is simply telling people that you're the authority on a certain subject, getting customers to believe you're an authority on that subject, and getting respected colleagues and industry professionals to also view you as an authority on the subject. One of the most obvious ways to gain credibility is to gather positive reviews and testimonials from past customers and clients and post them on your blog, your website, your Twitter account, your Facebook page, wherever you can. Just remember that the reviews or testimonials need to be real, meaning that they're from actual customers regarding an actual experience, and that you must obtain the customer's permission before you use them.

You don't need to rely on word of mouth of testimonials alone to build credibility. You can also proudly display the logo of any industry association that you belong to such as the Better Business Bureau, home associations, construction associations, or any other organizations in your field.

To build credibility, you also need to give your customers a sense that when they are on your site or blog, they are in a secure place. You can do this by having the security lock pad displayed at the bottom of the page on your site, the (s) that comes after the "http" in web addresses, showing that particular site is a secure site; or displaying security logos such as the McAfee logo.

# ORM Best Business Practices

*"As a general rule, a reputation is built on manner as much as on achievement."*
*Joseph Conrad*

Even though there's been a great deal about online reputation management covered in this report, chances are that you still have a lot of questions about your online reputation management.

Here are a few of the most common questions – and the answers to them:

### How important is customer privacy when it comes to my own online reputation?

This really goes without saying and it's brought up just to prove the point that you must always, always protect your customer's privacy. This means never selling or giving away information that they trust you with, whether it's their credit card number or their email address. You are *never* to give out information about your customers without their permission. No questions on that one.

### What policies should I have in place regarding managing my online reputation and social networking sites?

As mentioned earlier, you need to have policies and procedures in place for yourself and anyone else that publishes any content onto any of your company's social networking profiles. This will not only allow for regular, consistent content to be published, but it will also allow you to make sure that no offensive content is going up that could be damaging to your online reputation. Along with content policies, also make sure that your staff knows how to handle the privacy of friends and followers on those sites, as well as how to treat reviews, retweets, comments, videos, and images posted.

### How do I deal with a negative review?

If during your assessment of your online reputation you find negative reviews or comments, address them right then and there. Tell the person that you're sorry they feel that way and ask if there's anything you can do to help. Offer a comparative solution and make sure it's one that you can follow through on. Negative reviews don't have to be a terrible thing – they can be a terrific opportunity!

## Is it unethical to ask someone to remove a negative review?

Once you have taken care of the situation it's completely understandable and acceptable to ask the individual to remove the negative comment or review. They may surprise you and not only remove it, but write a positive review on how your company is willing to go above and beyond when it comes to customer satisfaction!

## How should I deal with false reviews?

So you've fixed a situation that actually happened and that you actually needed to make right. But what if there's information out there that's just blatantly *wrong* and *false?* This can be enraging when you're trying to build, protect, and manage your online reputation, but don't blow your top over it. Contact the individual or the website owner and let them know that the information they're displaying on their site is in fact, incorrect. Kindly ask them to remove the content and give them a few days to do so. If they haven't at that time, contact them again and be a bit firmer in your request, telling them that you will take further action if necessary. Usually, this is enough to get the content removed.

## What if it's not? Is legal action ever required?

Sometimes, but very rarely. If someone is publishing blatant lies about you and you've done everything you can to bring it to their attention and they *still* haven't listened, it might be worth your while to hire a lawyer and take legal action. Keep in mind though, that this should only be done in the most severe cases when slanderous things are being said and someone is doing a great deal of damage to your company's reputation. If it's not that severe, a lawsuit could follow your reputation for years to come and that could damage your online reputation even further. If the website owner won't remove the content and you don't feel as though legal action is necessary, remember that you can always write a review outlining that website and that false information. It does little to ease how upsetting the situation is, but sometimes biting your tongue will do more good than you know.

### Can I write my own reviews on my own company or product?

There is absolutely nothing wrong with writing your own reviews, but there is something wrong with writing your own reviews and saying that they were written by somebody else. If you write a review on your own product, be sure to say things like, "We're proud to say that our newest 6-man tent has features never seen in outdoor gear before." Never be misleading in your review and try to make people think that you're a customer that's actually used the product. It's simply unethical and there's nothing that will damage your credibility or your online reputation more than when customers find out that you lied in a review – and they will.

### Is it possible to have too many reviews?

Lots of people wonder if there can be too many reviews online about their company or product. There really is no such thing as too many positive reviews and you'll know if you're getting in too deep and in too much trouble with too many negative reviews. Generally, as long as you have four positive reviews for every one negative, you'll be fine.

### Is it ethical to buy followers on Facebook and Twitter?

It *is* possible to buy followers on many social networks, with Facebook and Twitter being the two biggest when it comes to this practice. Followers give you a leg up in search results, both on the social network and in Google, but the answer as to whether or not it's ethical is still up for debate. But even if there's absolutely nothing unethical about buying followers, it's something that shouldn't be done. "Ghost" followers offer little to contribute to your reputation and it can make your profile look as though just that – you've bought followers. In addition to that, when you buy followers, you don't always have the option of *who* you get. So on an English-speaking page you might get people speaking French, Spanish, Mandarin, or any other language. And people can't communicate, interact, and talk about your company if they don't understand each other.

### Where can I post reviews?

Posting reviews is different than posting general informative articles in article directories. To efficiently and effectively post a review of a product or your company try doing so on one of these sites: Google My Business, Yelp, CitySearch, MerchantCircle, Angie's List, and Insider Pages.

### Should I mention competitors in my reviews?

The days of it being illegal for one company to mention another by name are long gone, and people are free to say pretty much whatever they want about whoever they want – especially online. However, this doesn't mean that it's something you should do. While you should always try to convey to your customers that you have the best product and are the best company, you should be able to do that by pointing out what makes you so great – and not how bad your competition is. In fact, if you ever do mention your competition, it should be to recommend customers to them when you can't provide what they're looking for.

# Checklist: Questions to Ask

- ❑ What are the main things you will do to assess and build my online reputation?

- ❑ What social networking sites do you use, and will you use, to help build my online reputation?

- ❑ What sites would you be using to post reviews and articles about my company and product?

- ❑ Will you write my content for me?

- ❑ How will you track my online reputation?

- ❑ If those strategies don't work, will there be any compensation?

- ❑ What digital news do you subscribe to?

- ❑ What fees do you charge and what do those include? Will it include my online reputation management, and how much priority will you give that area in online marketing?

- ❑ Do you have references?

# Checklist: ORM Best Business Practices

❑ How important is customer privacy when it comes to my online reputation?

❑ What policies should I have in place regarding managing my online reputation and social networking sites?

❑ How do I deal with a negative review?

❑ Is it unethical to ask someone to remove a negative review?

❑ How should I deal with false reviews?

❑ Is legal action ever required?

❑ Can I write my own reviews on my own company or product?

❑ Is it possible to have too many reviews?

❑ Is it ethical to buy Facebook fans?

❑ Where can I post reviews?

❑ Should I mention competitors in my reviews?

# Next Steps

Get a personalized insight about your business digital presence related to:

- Online listing accuracy across review sites and directories
- Social media usage and influence
- Website responsiveness and SEO metrics
- SEM performance of online campaigns
- Local competitor analysis

To take advantage of this $250 value contact us at:

www.DoTheyReallyLikeMe.com

# About the Author

Randy Walden is known as an innovative and result –oriented Business Development Professional, acknowledged for well-defined understanding of business philosophy, developmental strategies, technology interface, and capacity to identify and align clients' needs with appropriate products and services.

Randy has a successful and diverse background spanning Business Development, Marketing, Sales, operational management, technical support within the corporate enterprise with expertise in engaging key partners and devising winning sales strategies and solutions to increase revenue and enhance productivity. Maintain business-focused value propositions that leverage competitive advantage via top quality service. Skilled in optimizing team's dynamics, uniting diverse agendas to a common goal, and harnessing strategic and operational drivers to deliver results.

www.ingramcontent.com/pod-product-compliance
Lightning Source LLC
Chambersburg PA
CBHW071545170526
45166CB00004B/1558